The *"Faith in Action"* Series
General Editors: *Geoffrey Hanks and
David Wallington*

CHILDREN OF NAPLES

THE STORY OF PASTOR SANTI

Geoffrey Hanks

THE RELIGIOUS EDUCATION PRESS

A member of the Pergamon Group

A. Wheaton and Company (Educational Publishers),
Hennock Road, Exeter EX2 8RP.

Pergamon of Canada Ltd., P.O Box 9600, Don Mills,
Ontario M3C 2T9, Canada.

Pergamon Press (Aust.) Pty Ltd., 19a Boundary Street,
Rushcutters Bay, N.S.W. 2011, Australia.

Cover photograph of Naples by courtesy of Picturepoint Ltd.

First edition 1974
Reprinted 1975

Printed in Great Britain by A. Wheaton & Co., Exeter

ISBN 0 08 017618 6 non net
ISBN 0 08 017619 4 net

CHILDREN OF NAPLES

The story of Pastor Santi

It was Riccardo Santi's thirty-fourth birthday. His wife was busy preparing a treat and it would be some time before the tea was ready.

"Why don't you go out for a walk until tea is ready?" his wife suggested.

Taking the hint Riccardo wandered into the main streets of Naples, killing time until the meal was ready. As he walked the streets that afternoon he began to notice more than ever before the poverty of the city. There were lots of children hanging about in the streets, with apparently nothing better to do. They were thin and looked as if nobody cared for them. The houses were old and falling down—badly in need of repairs and a coat of paint.

Suddenly, a small, shrill voice awakened him. "Matches? Buy some matches. Matches, mister?" pleaded a boy.

Riccardo looked around to find a small boy holding out a box of matches for him to buy. With the boy was an even younger girl, obviously his sister. They were very poor and were shivering—not from cold, but from hunger and fear.

"Who are you?" asked Riccardo.

"My name is Antonio," replied the boy. "And my sister is called Maria. Buy a box of matches, please."

Pastor Santi and children.

But Pastor Santi, the minister of the Methodist Church in Naples (Italy) was not to be put off, and went on with his questions.

"Where do you live?" he asked.

"We don't have a home now," answered Antonio. "Sometimes we sleep under the stairs at the railway station, and sometimes just out in the open."

"What about your parents?" the pastor went on.

"We don't have a father—he died last week, and mother works as a servant in a big house. She'll come to fetch us when it's dark."

At this point Riccardo's mind went back to his own childhood. His father had died when Riccardo was only five years old. His mother was too poor to look after him. At the age of seven he had been placed in a children's home. Although the food had been plain and the discipline strict, the boys in the children's home had received all the love and the help that was needed.

Now God seemed to be speaking to him, telling him to do the same for these youngsters.

"These children belong to Me. Take them and love them for My sake. Do for them what was done for you when you were a child; I will supply the means and I will bless you." It was to Riccardo the clear command of God to take these children to his home, and he obeyed.

"Well, it's my birthday today," explained the pastor to the children, "and I want you to come to tea with me." With that he took the two youngsters by the hand and led the way back to his home.

It wasn't the first time that the pastor had taken unexpected guests back to his home, and his wife was getting quite used to it. Naples was full of beggars and people in rags, and the Methodist Church had become a centre where the homeless could find shelter, even if the beds were only hard benches.

When Riccardo presented himself and his guests to his wife, ready for the party, she knew what to expect. There was barely enough to go round for her own family, without having two more to feed. Antonio and Maria looked at the food on the table as though they hadn't eaten for days— probably they hadn't.

Even though there was not much, the food was divided and shared around to everyone.

After tea Riccardo and his wife discussed what ought to be done. His salary was so small that it was hardly enough for his own family, let alone two extra children.

At last it was decided that the two children should stay— "Just for tonight." The children's mother was found and she readily gave her permission.

And so the two children stayed for the night . . . and for the next . . . and the next! Without realising it Pastor Santi had begun his children's home.

The year was 1905.

The rent is paid

The Methodist Church in Naples is in one of the poorer districts of the city. The streets are narrow and dark, the tall buildings shutting out most of the light.

The church wasn't a building of the kind we know; it was simply a large room on the ground floor of a three-storeyed building. There was no pulpit, just a few wooden benches and a plain wooden table for Holy Communion.

Most people in Italy are Roman Catholic. The Methodist Church of Italy in those days consisted of only a few hundred members, and so to be a Methodist made you someone rather different.

The following Sunday Pastor Santi shared the problem with his few people. "If God wants us to keep these children," he explained to his members, "He will supply all the things we need. What do you think?"

They replied by bringing gifts, and before the Sunday was over Pastor Santi had received food, clothing, a table, some bedding and a little money. Enough, in fact, to care for the two extra children for more than a month! The pastor knew how poor his people were and that they really could not afford to give these things. "The Lord has blessed us," he said. But their troubles were only just beginning. As the news spread around, more homeless children found their way to the Santis' house. Some were brought in by the neighbours and some by the pastor. All the children were somehow squeezed into the small flat where the Santi family lived. To help out, all the tasks of the home were shared around—Mama did the cooking, Papa cut the boys' hair and looked after their illnesses, while the older girls helped with mending the clothes.

The size of the family further increased when the volcano Vesuvius erupted, making more children homeless. Pastor Santi's salary of 90 lire a month, together with the help of his church, was still not enough to meet the needs of all the family. The day came when there was no money to pay the rent. Although the landlord admired the good work Pastor Santi was doing, it didn't meet the debt.

"If the rent isn't paid by tomorrow, you will all be turned out into the streets," he threatened.

That night, as always, the pastor shared the problem with the family at their evening prayers.

"Why not sell off some of the furniture?" suggested one of the older children.

First, however, they turned their need into a prayer and told God all about their problem. Suddenly, in the middle of their prayers, there was a voice at the door, asking for Pastor Santi. When the pastor answered the door he recognised the caller as a man who had been in his church several Sundays before. He remembered him clearly, as the pastor appeared to have upset him by something he said in his sermon, and the man had stormed out of the church in a rage.

"I am sorry I behaved so badly in church," apologised the visitor. Having said this he placed an envelope in Riccardo's hand.

"Please accept this gift as my way of saying sorry," he said, and with that he left.

The pastor opened the envelope. He gasped in surprise as he drew out a small bundle of notes.

"God has already answered our prayers," he told the family. "He has sent us much more money than we need, so you can all sleep soundly in your beds tonight." The envelope contained enough money to pay the rent for a whole year!

A palace for a home

The number of children continued to increase and the Santis were at last forced to move to a bigger flat. A second volcano disaster, this time in Sicily, brought another group of homeless children into the family, bringing the total to over fifty, so that even with the extra space all the room was taken up.

It was at this time, during the First World War when Italy was on the side of Britain, that Riccardo Santi's work came to the notice of the Methodist Church in America. The church gave him enough money to buy a four-storeyed building, near the city centre, but this did not have all the necessary space. "How much money do you want, then?" they asked the pastor. The pastor thought and replied, "I don't want any money."

The Americans were surprised!

"No money?" they gasped. "Well, what do you want?"

"I want a house—a house big enough for all my children, a house big enough for me to have a school, and where the children have enough space to run about and be free."

Vitamin tablets for the little ones.

"You shall have your house," was the promise.

It was not until a year later, in 1919, that the plan began to take shape. In that year a group of American Methodists paid another visit to Italy, to help Pastor Santi buy a house for use as a children's home.

The Americans took Riccardo on a tour of the city of Naples, looking at all the houses that seemed the right size. The taxi-driver was patient, taking them from one building to another, but in vain; either the houses were far too expensive or they simply were not the right sort of building for a children's home.

Just when they were about to give up, the taxi-driver, who by now was listening to all their talk and taking a real interest in the search, broke into the conversation.

"Why don't you try Portici?" he suggested. "There's a large house for sale there, and it's by the sea."

So it was that the taxi-driver turned the car round and was soon rattling along the cobbled streets of this suburb of Naples. Portici lies south of Naples on the road out to Sorrento. Once it had been a village on the King of Naples' estate; now it was one of the poorest parts of the city, rapidly becoming a slum.

After a short while the taxi turned off the main street, through a large gateway, into a quiet courtyard. A drive, lined with palm trees, led up to what had obviously once been a building of some splendour.

The group of visitors got out of the taxi and looked around. Behind them, not too far away, rose the heights of Mt. Vesuvius, the volcano; beyond the house, the blue Mediterranean Sea, a mere 100 yards away.

They inspected the two buildings and looked around the grounds.

"It's got just about everything we want," exclaimed Riccardo excitedly. "Big buildings, plenty of space and a

The school band in front of the Casa Materna. The Italian words above the entrance come from the gospel: "Let the children come to me".

farm—more than enough for the children to play around in."

"Would you like it?" asked the Americans.

"Would there be enough money to buy it?" asked the pastor.

"All we want is to buy the place you need—leave the matter of the money to us," was the reply.

It was Easter 1920 when the 80 children, together with the Santi family, moved into their royal home. Repairs had to be made—woodwork needed painting, the gardens to be dug over; at first, sufficient only was done to make the

9

removal possible. They named their palace Casa Materna, which means 'Mother's Home'.

Portici had only one school and there was no chance of all the children getting in. Riccardo Santi always paid great attention to the children's education, so Mama Santi, with the help of her eldest daughter Luisa, had to organise her own classes. When the Santi 'school' was set up, the local children began to ask if they could come as well. In a matter of years the numbers in the school had risen to over 300, which included 100 from Casa Materna.

Arrested by the Fascists

In 1922 Mussolini seized power and became a Dictator (or 'Leader') like Hitler. He ruled Italy, supported by his small band of followers called Fascists, until he was shot in 1945.

Because of the evil deeds of the Fascists Riccardo Santi opposed them, so they began to look for ways of dealing with him. On one occasion he was arrested by the secret police and accused of being a traitor. His 'crime' was that he had visited the aged parents of a man hunted by the Fascists, to tell them that their son was alive and well. On another occasion he was arrested and accused of being a spy.

His third arrest came in 1938. One day a large car escorted by a motor-cyclist drew up outside the door of the Home. It came to take the pastor to jail.

The following day, along with a group of criminals, he was tried in court.

"Riccardo Santi, you are accused of preaching strange doctrines," was the charge.

The officer of the court then began to fire questions at

him. But every time the pastor tried to answer the question the officer told him to be quiet! Finally came a question to which Riccardo managed a reply—

"What do you preach?" he was asked.

Seizing the opportunity, Riccardo pulled a Bible from his pocket and began to explain the gospel to him, turning from one verse to another. The officer of the court tried several times to interrupt the sermon, but the pastor would not stop until he had finished all he wanted to say.

Then the officer made yet another mistake; not having learnt his lesson he next asked Riccardo an even more dangerous question—

"What else do you do at Casa Materna, besides preach?"

"I pray, like this," he replied. And putting his hands together and closing his eyes, he began quietly to pray. The people in the courtroom stared at him in disbelief, as the pastor prayed for the poor, for those on trial, for the rulers of the nation and for the magistrates themselves. He thanked God for his daily mercies and above all for his love. The police officers stood there embarrassed, not knowing what to do.

The officer of the court rose to his feet, his face red with anger.

"Throw this man out of court," he shouted. And Riccardo Santi left the court a free man.

Casa Materna saved from the Germans

By now, 1939, Hitler had drawn all Europe into war. Mussolini joined forces with Hitler, and Europe became a huge battleground.

There were several attempts made during these years to close down Casa Materna. In 1943, for example, a group of German army officers visited the Home with a view to taking it over as their new military headquarters. The children had been moved out into the country for safety, and so the buildings were no longer in use as a Home. Use by the army would have made Casa Materna a military target, and that might well have been the end of all Pastor Santi's work.

The major in charge of the party took the keys and began an inspection of the buildings, leaving a young officer in the hall with one of Pastor Santi's sons, a young man called Teofilo.

As he wandered around the entrance hall the officer read a notice on one of the walls, which stated that Casa Materna was a gift from the Methodist Church of America. The officer, who could only understand a little English, asked Teofilo, "Why is the word 'Methodist' here?"

"Because this building was given to us by the Methodists of America," came the reply.

"Then you are a Methodist?" asked the officer.

"Yes," replied Teofilo.

At this, the officer shook him firmly by the hand and said, "I, too, am a Methodist."

"In that case, try and save this building for us," pleaded Teofilo. "If it becomes the German headquarters it will be bombed."

The officer went off to find the major, promising to do what he could. A short while later the group of visitors returned, the major shaking his head.

"I'm afraid this place won't do," he said. "This officer has pointed out that the buildings would be difficult to camouflage, and that the roadway between the two buildings could easily be spotted from the air."

With that, the group of officers got back into the car and drove away. So not *all* Germans were like Hitler!

12

After the war

During the war the children were moved to a small village called Praiano, about 40 miles from Naples. There they stayed until our soldiers forced Italy to surrender in September 1943. But Casa Materna was now occupied by British troops. Also it had been damaged during the war, so that it was not until October 1944 that the children were able to move back to their old home.

The gardens were a jungle of weeds and pitted with bomb craters. At first the children lived in out-buildings or in tents, whilst the job of restoring the buildings went ahead.

Pastor Santi was by now over 70 years old and the job of running the Home was being taken over more and more by one of his sons, Fabio.

Fabio was a lawyer. He stood over 6 ft. tall—a big man with a big heart. Such was his popularity in Portici that he was later elected Mayor, a great honour for a Methodist. Just after the war, however, Naples was occupied by the Americans, and Fabio decided to ask them for help.

One day, for example, he brought an American Chaplain to look over Casa Materna. When the Chaplain saw the needs of the children he reported the situation to his colonel. Result: a truckful of bread and beefsteak was immediately sent for the children.

Later, an American soldier drove into the Home with a load of old tents.

"Fabio," he called out. "Do you want a load of old tents for the kids?"

"No thanks," came the reply, "we've finished sleeping in tents now the buildings have been repaired."

"They may be no use as tents," said the soldier, "but they would make far better blouses for the girls than the ones they are wearing."

And so the tents were made into blouses!

As life returned to normal it was felt that the school should be re-opened. So Pastor Santi and his wife went round the houses of Portici, inviting the children back to the school. The first day about 60 children turned up for lessons to join the 100 or so from Casa Materna.

Today there are over 400 children at the school, housed in a new school block.

Everything possible is done to help the boys and girls prepare for the time when they will leave school to go out to work. Most of the courses are practical, that is in subjects where the children learn to use their hands. There are workshops for the boys, and the girls are taught catering, typewriting and similar subjects.

A visit to America

Music has always played an important part in the life of the Santi family. Mama Santi was an excellent pianist and taught all her children to play the piano, as well as to enjoy singing. One of the Santi sons, Emanuele, went to America and became a famous violinist.

But one of the outstanding memories of Casa Materna is the choir, which came into being almost by accident.

It happened like this.

Joel Warner was a young American who had come to Casa Materna to spend a short while helping out. Somehow, he didn't seem to fit in and there was nothing he seemed to be able to put his hand to. Until one day Fabio heard voices singing in the Music Room. To his surprise he discovered that Joel not only had muscial talent, but was able to get the children singing in such a way as they had never sung before.

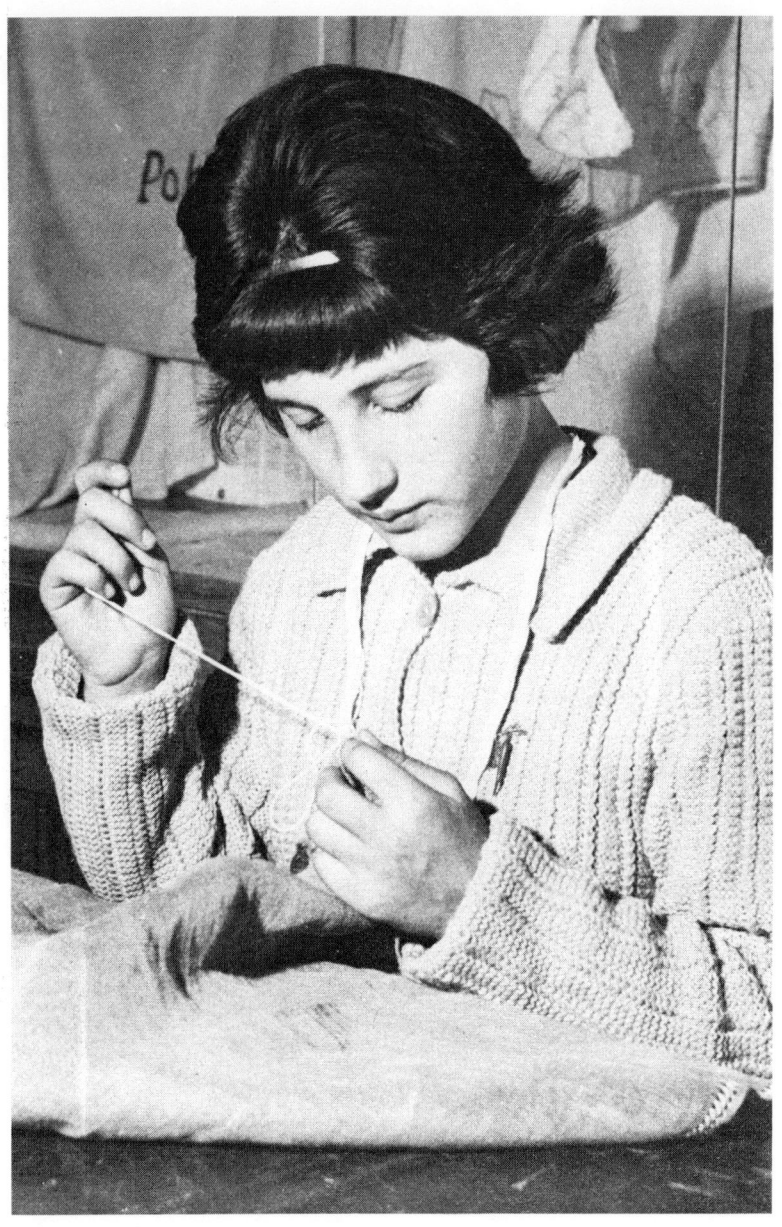

One of the girls doing embroidery.

"Why don't we form a choir?" suggested Joel. "Then we could give a few concerts and raise some money for the Home."

So the choir was formed. This was in 1955. In the following year Fabio and a group of 34 boys and girls set sail for America, to give a series of concerts. The cost of the tour was over £5,000, but the choir received much more than that from the people who came to hear them.

Wherever they went they were received with enthusiasm. They gave over 110 concerts, as well as making several recordings.

Then came tragedy. First, when the choir was almost at the end of its tour, a telegram was received saying that Mama Santi had died. Fabio and the children were heartbroken and longed to be back home. The tour was a success—there was now enough money to begin building new sleeping quarters for the children.

When the boat taking the children back to Naples drew into port there were hundreds of friends there to greet them. TV cameras and reporters were all there to record their return.

But one person was missing, and the last song of the tour was sung at the graveside of Mama Santi.

Then three months after the concert tour ended, Fabio was killed in a road accident while driving to Rome. No one ever knew how it happened, but his car swerved across the empty road and hit a post. He died instantly.

Pastor Santi lived on a few more years and died in 1961, just before his 90th birthday.

Now the work of the Home is managed by the two remaining brothers, Teofilo and Emanuele.

*   *   *   *

Fabio and the choir mapping out their American tour.

Throughout its history Casa Materna has taken as its motto the words of Jesus, when He said, "Let the children come to Me." Never has a single child in need of help ever been turned away. Pastor Santi always used to say that the greatest gift he could give a child was love.

"I do not ask myself whether a child is suffering, but I become that child," he frequently explained. By this he meant that he put himself in the place of every child in need whom he met.

Mama Santi, too, loved the children just as much. Many years ago a friend of Casa Materna wrote these words about her:

"With such love does this fine person go about her work that at first I could not distinguish between her own children and those who were adopted."

This, then, is the Casa Materna story. It is not yet finished, for the task of providing a 'Mother's Home' still goes on.

BIOGRAPHICAL NOTES

Riccardo Santi was born in Bologna (northern Italy) in the year 1871. His father was a carpenter, and a Roman Catholic. Through reading a Bible he came to a personal faith in Jesus Christ. He then joined the Methodist Church.

When Riccardo was only five years old his father died, leaving his widow to bring up their three sons. The burden was too much, and in 1878 when Riccardo was seven years old he was sent to a Methodist Home for boys, in Venice.

At the age of twenty-one Riccardo Santi felt called by God to become a Methodist Minister, and he went to Rome to do his training.

In 1897 he married Ersilia Bragaglia, who had trained as a concert pianist. Together they went to Bari (southern Italy) to take charge of a small church.

In 1903 Riccardo was sent to be the pastor of the Methodist Church in Naples, which proved to be the Santis' home for the rest of their lives.

There were four children born to Riccardo and Ersilia Santi: Fabio, who became a lawyer; Emanuele, a concert violinist; Teofilo, a doctor, and their sister, Luisa.

ACKNOWLEDGEMENT

The author wishes to thank the Rev Cyril Davey for permission to use material from his book, *The Santi Story*, published by Epworth Press (hard cover) and by Marshall, Morgan and Scott (paper back), and Dr Emanuele Santi of Casa Materna for the loan of photographs.

THINGS TO DO

A Test yourself

Here are some short questions. See if you can remember the answers from what you have read. Then write them down in a few words.

1. Why did Pastor Santi take Antonio and Maria to live at his home?
2. In what way did these two children remind him of his own childhood?
3. Which sort of Church did the Pastor belong to?
4. What does the name 'Casa Materna' mean?
5. Give one reason why the Pastor was once arrested.
6. Why was he thrown out of court?
7. What happened to Casa Materna during the war?
8. How was the choir able to help raise money for the Home?
9. What lessons do the children have at the Casa Materna school to prepare them for the time when they go out to work?
10. What is the Casa Materna motto?

B Think through

These questions need longer answers. Think about them, then try to write two or three sentences in answer to each one. You may look up the story again to help you.

1. Explain the reasons why Pastor Santi began his work among the children of Naples.
2. Describe any one incident from the story that shows the Pastor's faith.
3. How were other Methodists able to help the work of the Home?

C To talk about

Here are some questions for you to talk about with each other. Try to give reasons for what you say or think.
Try to find out all the different opinions which people have about each question.

1 Are Children's Homes still needed today? Can a Children's Home take the place of a real home and family?

2 If you were running a school, which subjects would you include on the time-table? Why?

3 Pastor Santi was brought up in a Children's Home where the *discipline* was strict and yet where he claimed he received all the *love* that he needed. Is it possible to be strict and also to show love?

4 Jesus said, "Let the children come to Me." What do you think this means?

D Find out

Choose one or two of the subjects below and find out all you can about them. History books, geography books and newspapers may be useful. Perhaps you can also use reference books in your library to look up some of the names and places. You can illustrate the work with your own drawings.

1 *Naples and southern Italy.* Use a geography book and an atlas:
   (a) Draw a map of Italy and Sicily, and put on Naples and Rome, Mount Vesuvius and Mount Etna.
   (b) Find out what work the people of southern Italy do, and why they are so poor.
   (c) Read the story of Father Borrelli's work amongst the children of Naples and then write an account.
   (d) How many times is Mount Vesuvius known to have erupted? Find out about the eruption which buried the town of Pompeii.

2 *Children's Homes.* The following men have also founded Homes: Dr. Barnardo, George Müller (Bristol), Dr. Stephenson (National Children's Homes), and Charles Spurgeon (London, now in Kent). Look up any one of these in your own school library and write a short account of the work.

3 *The Methodist Church.* Find out all you can about the Methodist Church: how it started, what the Church does and what its members believe. Begin your work by finding out all you can about John and Charles Wesley.

4 *The Fascists.* What is a Fascist? Find out about the career of Mussolini, the Italian Fascist leader.

USEFUL INFORMATION

Addresses:

Italian State Tourist
   Department,
201 Regent Street,
London, W.1.

Dr. Barnardo's,
Tanner's Lane,
Barkingside, Essex.

Methodist Education
   Committee,
25 Marylebone Road,
London, N.W.1.

National Children's Home,
85 Highbury Park,
London, N.5.

Casa Materna,
235 Corso Garibaldi,
1 80055 Portici,
Naples, Italy.

George Müller Homes,
Müller House,
7 Cotham Park,
Bristol BS6 6DA.

N.B. Remember to enclose a stamped addressed envelope for the reply.

More books to read

Take This Child—The Santi Story, by Cyril Davey (Marshall, Morgan and Scott).
John Wesley and Methodism—A Guide for Schools, by Thomas Shaw (Wesley Historical Society, from the Epworth Press).
The Defiant Ones, by Brian Peachment (Religious Education Press), for the story of Father Borrelli.
A Man for all Children, by Cyril Davey (Epworth Press), the story of Dr. Stephenson.
Father of Nobody's Children, by Norman Wymer (Arrow Books, from Dr. Barnardo's).

Films

The Bay of Naples Tour (Italian State Tourist Dept.).

Naples, the Anonymous, on the work of Father Borrelli (House of the Urchins Fund, 19 Rodger Drive, Rutherglen, Glasgow).

The George Müller Story (Religious Films Ltd., 6 Eaton Gate, London, S.W.1).

Within Our Gates (Spurgeon's Homes, 25 Haddon House, Park Road, Birchington, Kent).

Filmstrip

Dr. Barnardo, Common Ground Filmstrips, Longman Group Ltd., Pinnacles, Harlow, Essex.